DINOSAUR WORLD
Stiff Armor
The Adventure of Ankylosaurus

Written by Michael Dahl

Illustrated by Garry Nichols

Special thanks to our advisers for their expertise:

Content Adviser: Philip J. Currie, Curator of Dinosaurs,
Royal Tyrrell Museum of Palaeontology, Drumheller, Alberta, Canada

Reading Adviser: Susan Kesselring, M.A., Literacy Educator,
Rosemount - Apple Valley - Eagan (Minnesota) School District

PICTURE WINDOW BOOKS
Minneapolis, Minnesota

Managing Editor: Catherine Neitge
Creative Director: Terri Foley
Art Director: Keith Griffin
Editor: Patricia Stockland
Designer: Joe Anderson
Page production: Picture Window Books
The illustrations in this book were prepared digitally.

Picture Window Books
5115 Excelsior Boulevard
Suite 232
Minneapolis, MN 55416
877-845-8392
www.picturewindowbooks.com

Printed in the United States of America.

Library of Congress Cataloging-in-Publication Data
Dahl, Michael.
Stiff armor : the adventure of Ankylosaurus / written by
Michael Dahl ; illustrated by Garry Nichols.
p. cm. — (Dinosaur world)
Includes bibliographical references and index.
ISBN 1-4048-0938-4 (hardcover)
ISBN 1-4048-1837-5 (paperback)
1. Ankylosaurus—Juvenile literature. I. Nichols, Garry, 1958-
ill. II. Title.

QE862.O65D33 2004
567.915—dc22   2004018917

No humans lived during the time of the dinosaurs. No person heard them roar, saw their scales, or felt their feathers.

The giant creatures are gone, but their fossils, or remains, lie hidden in the earth. Dinosaur skulls, skeletons, and eggs have been buried in rock for millions of years.

All around the world, scientists dig up fossils and carefully study them. Bones show how tall the dinosaurs stood. Claws and teeth show how they grabbed and what they ate. Scientists compare fossils with the bodies of living creatures such as birds and reptiles, which are relatives of the dinosaurs. Every year, scientists learn more and more about the giants that have disappeared.

Studying fossils and figuring out how the dinosaurs lived is like putting together the pieces of a puzzle that is millions of years old.

This is what some of those pieces can tell us about the dinosaur known as *Ankylosaurus* (ANG-kuh-loh-sawr-us).

Ankylosaurus bent its heavy, bony head over a stream. Water lilies floated near the shore. Soft green moss covered the gently sloping bank.

4

Buzz! Zzzz! *Ankylosaurus* turned toward the sound. Insects surrounded a cluster of magnolias. The pink and yellow blossoms filled the warm air with a sweet scent. *Ankylosaurus* moved toward the flowers.

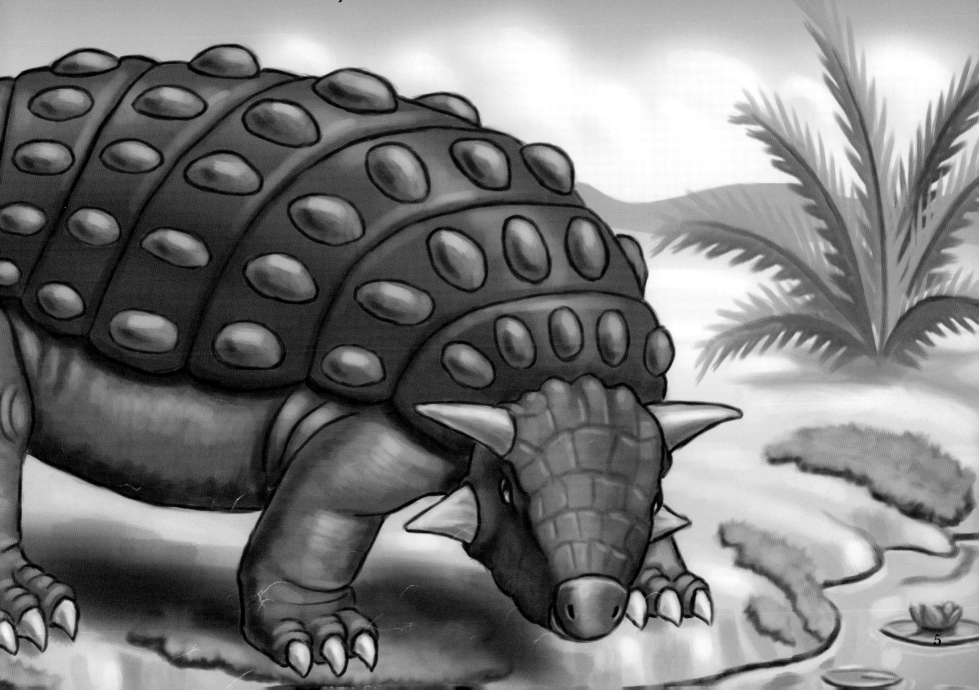

Ankylosaurus munched the magnolia petals. The dinosaur's small teeth ripped the flowers off the branches. Its thick tongue curled around the tender green leaves.

As *Anklyosaurus* ate more and more of the blossoms, the buzzing insects flew off.

Ankylosaurus was an herbivore, a plant-eating dinosaur. Because of its low, heavy body, the dinosaur grazed on plants that grew close to the ground. It spent almost all day filling its enormous belly with moss, ferns, flowers, and leaves.

7

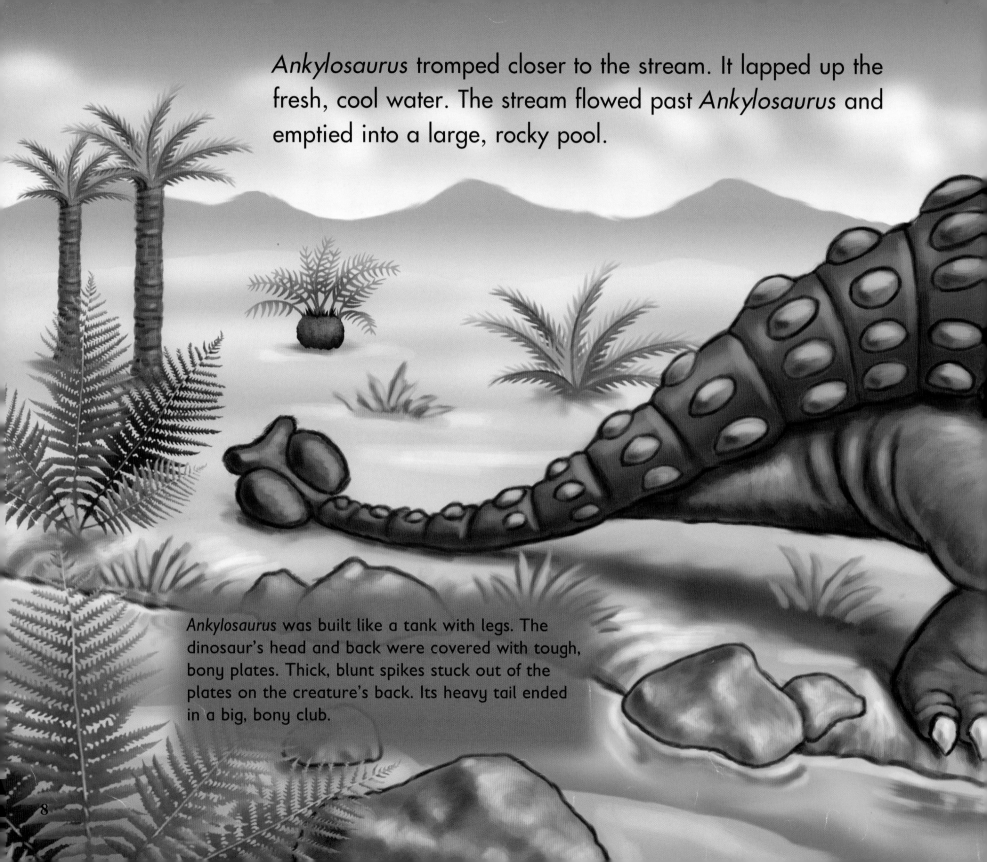

Ankylosaurus tromped closer to the stream. It lapped up the fresh, cool water. The stream flowed past *Ankylosaurus* and emptied into a large, rocky pool.

Ankylosaurus was built like a tank with legs. The dinosaur's head and back were covered with tough, bony plates. Thick, blunt spikes stuck out of the plates on the creature's back. Its heavy tail ended in a big, bony club.

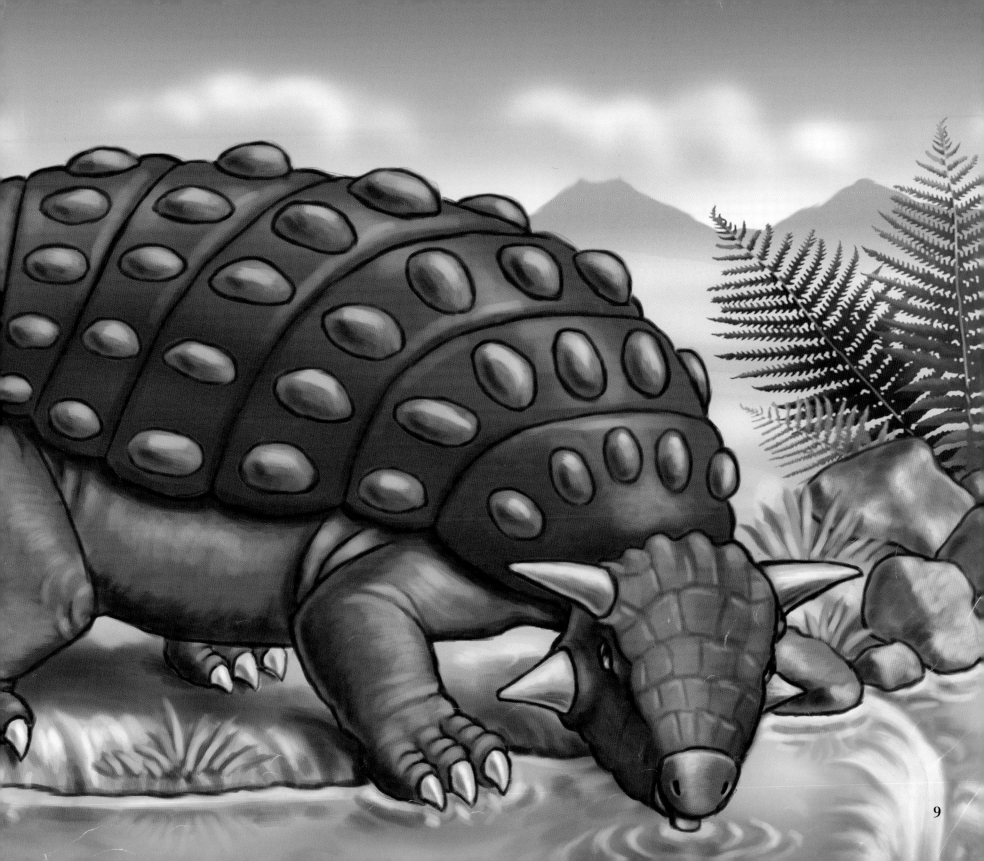

Thunder rumbled overhead, but the sun was shining. No rain clouds hung in the sky. *Ankylosaurus* saw a red glow in the distance.

A volcano erupted. The mountain was pouring hot, thick smoke into the air. Fiery rocks and hot ash began to fall in the stream. *Ankylosaurus* plunged into the water and waded through the pool.

Ankylosaurus was a heavy, low-built dinosaur that looked like a giant armadillo. Many scientists believe the bulky Ankylosaurus moved very slowly.

11

Ankylosaurus left the stream. It charged through the burning ferns and bushes. As the creature rumbled over the ground, it lowered its thick eyelids, protecting its eyes against the falling ash.

The sky grew darker. The sun was blocked out by thick clouds shooting from the volcano.

The plates that covered *Ankylosaurus*'s body even grew inside its eyelids. The thick lids opened and shut over the eyes like tiny window shutters. *Ankylosaurus* probably had small eyes and couldn't see well in the dark.

13

As *Ankylosaurus* moved through the forest, it heard other creatures crashing through the trees and bushes. Loud cries and roars drowned out the rumbling volcano.

Ankylosaurus stopped quickly. Its hoof-like claws dug into the dirt. Blocking the plant-eater's path stood another dinosaur that fled from the falling ash. Tall, deadly *Tyrannosaurus rex* blinked at *Ankylosaurus*. The meat-eater clicked its fearsome claws.

Ankylosaurus had dangerous neighbors. Predators prowled through forests and lurked in swamps. Some of the meat-eaters were called raptors. One of the creatures that hunted *Ankylosaurus* for food was *Tyrannosaurus rex*. *Tyrannosaurus* means "tyrant lizard."

15

Ankylosaurus was much shorter and slower than *Tyrannosaurus rex*. The armored dinosaur turned around to flee the predator. More terrible roars came from behind a wall of ferns.

The ferns parted and out hopped three small raptors. They were frightened by the volcano's smoke and thunder. The raptors snapped their jaws at *Ankylosaurus*.

Most meat-eaters stayed away from *Ankylosaurus*. The dinosaur's tough armor and sharp spikes were good protection. The only part of the creature's body that was not protected was its soft underbelly. If a predator could flip *Ankylosaurus* on its back, the plant-eater was doomed.

17

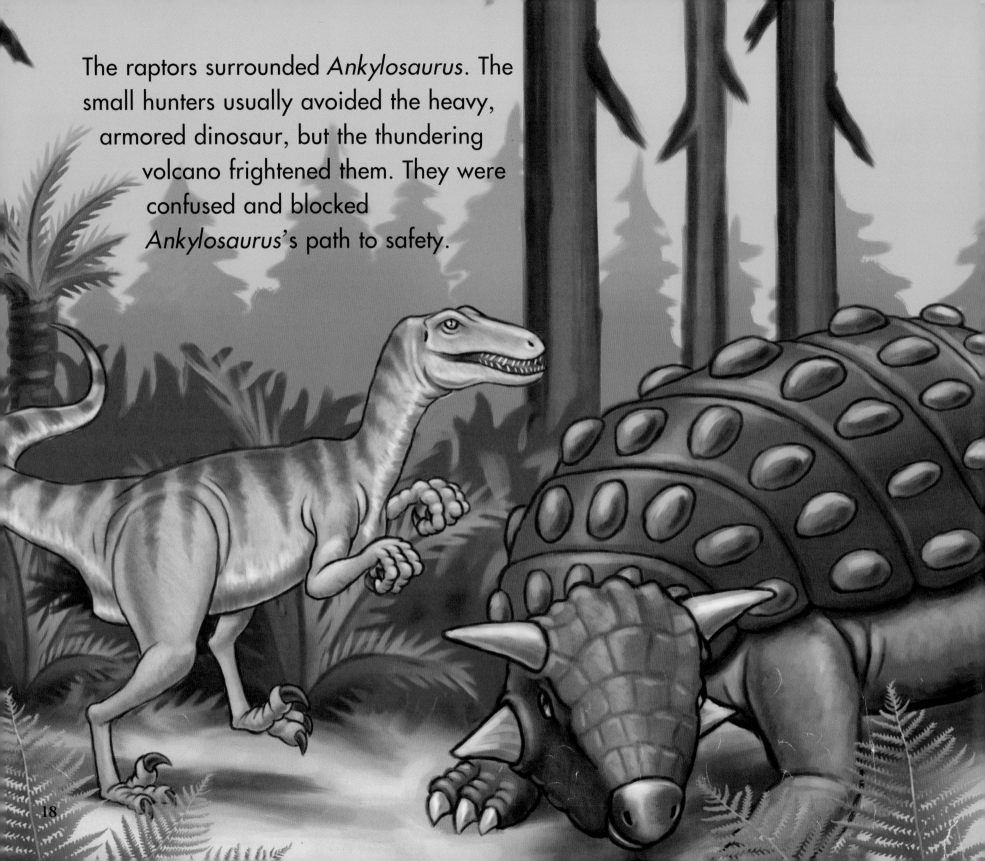

The raptors surrounded *Ankylosaurus*. The small hunters usually avoided the heavy, armored dinosaur, but the thundering volcano frightened them. They were confused and blocked *Ankylosaurus*'s path to safety.

Ankylosaurus bent its head. The dinosaur turned, swinging its heavy tail at the nearest predator. Crack! The tail club broke a raptor's leg. The creature howled with pain.

Ankylosaurus was armed with a massive, club-like tail. The rounded knob at the end of the tail was made of several thick, bony plates. Most scientists believe the tail was powerful enough to break through bone.

19

The raptor lay on its back, surrounded by the falling, flaming ash. The other raptors ran away. *Tyrannosaurus rex* eyed the helpless raptor. It would not let a volcano stand in the way of a crunchy snack.

Ankylosaurus lowered it heavy lids once more. It took a deep breath. The armored plant-eater headed into the ferns, escaping the hungry *Tyrannosaurus rex* and the volcano's flames and smoke.

Ankylosaurus: Where ...

Ankylosaurus fossils have been found around the world: Alberta, Canada, and Montana and Wyoming in the United States.

... and When

The "Age of Dinosaurs" began 248 million years ago (mya). If we imagine the time from the beginning of the dinosaur age to the present as one day, the Age of Dinosaurs lasted 18 hours—and humans have only been around for 10 minutes!

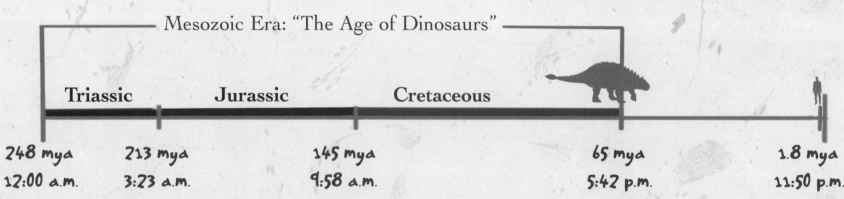

Mesozoic Era: "The Age of Dinosaurs"

Triassic	Jurassic	Cretaceous

248 mya	213 mya	145 mya	65 mya	1.8 mya
12:00 a.m.	3:23 a.m.	9:58 a.m.	5:42 p.m.	11:50 p.m.

Triassic—Dinosaurs first appear. Early mammals appear.
Jurassic—First birds appear.
Cretaceous—Flowering plants appear. By the end of this era, all dinosaurs disappear.

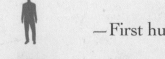
—First humans appear

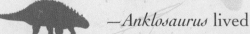
—*Anklosaurus* lived

22

Digging Deeper

Stinky Gas

Ankylosaurus ate plants all day long. To help digest all that food, the dinosaur may have had a special chamber in its large gut. Scientists think the chamber had chemicals that dissolved and digested the food. This "fermentation" chamber also produced lots and lots of gas. *Ankylosaurus* was probably a very smelly creature!

Many Meanings

Like many other dinosaurs, *Ankylosaurus* was given a name using ancient Greek words. "Saurus" comes from the Greek word meaning "lizard." But the word "ankylo" can mean several things. It can mean "bent," referring to *Ankylosaurus*'s hunched-over posture. It can mean "stiff," describing the hard, bony back and spikes. Or it can mean "fused," or blended together. The armor plates on *Ankylosaurus* did not sit on its back like a turtle's shell. Instead, the plates were blended into the dinosaur's leathery skin.

High Tail

Ankylosaurus's tail was a powerful weapon. Some scientists believe it would have been strong enough to punch through a house. Powerful back muscles controlled the tail. When it walked, *Ankylosaurus* probably held the heavy tail several feet above the ground. It was always ready to swing.

Champion Chewers

For a long time, scientists thought that *Ankylosaurus* did not have very good teeth. They figured *Ankylosaurus* ate its food like other plant-eaters. Those creatures swallowed small stones, called gastroliths, which ground up food inside the dinosaur's belly. Now, scientists have learned that *Ankylosaurus* had strong, leaf-shaped teeth in the sides of its mouth. These teeth were excellent at shredding and chewing up tough plants without the use of stones.

Words to Know

armor—protective covering on an animal

carnivore—a creature that eats only meat, or other living creatures

dinosaurs—giant creatures that lived millions of years ago; scientists think that many modern reptiles and birds are related to dinosaurs

herbivore—a creature that eats only plants

predator—a creature that hunts other animals for food

prey—an animal that is hunted and eaten by other animals

To Learn More

At the Library

Benton, Michael. *Armored Giants*. Brookfield, Conn.: Copper Beech Books, 2001.

Cohen, Daniel. *Ankylosaurus*. Mankato, Minn.: Bridgestone Books, 2003.

Schomp, Virginia. *Ankylosaurus: And Other Armored Plant-eaters*. New York: Benchmark Books, 2003.

On the Web

FactHound offers a safe, fun way to find Web sites related to this book. All of the sites on FactHound have been researched by our staff. *www.facthound.com*

1. Visit the FactHound home page.
2. Enter a search word related to this book, or type in this special code: 1404809384
3. Click on the FETCH IT button.

Your trusty FactHound will fetch the best Web sites for you!